T0288050

C

O

CONFLICT

N   Norman Fischer

F

L

I

C

T   chax press 2012

ISBN 978 0925904 72 0

Chax Press
411 N 7th Ave Ste 103
Tucson, Arizona 85705-8388

Printed in the United States of America

Acknowledgments:
A selection of these poems appeard in Volt magazine.
Thanks to Gillian Conoley.

to GaryFriedman, Jack Himmelstein

to students of the Center for Understanding in Conflict

to soldiers and other victims of war

... key words , elasticized phrases

... elephantine sensibilities kept me awake all night

heartache stirs my fears

I need an anti-inflammatory .... something... anything...

as quick as my fingers can grip the doorknob I'm out of here

just another stark arrangement

"this whole thing's a dark experiment"

what judgment ? whose ? where and why ? what are we talking about ?

"that bastard!"   *" if I could I would..."*

   but if I did

  where would I be

&

where would I be after that

–   how my fingers

  grip it

      how firmly shut it is

is there a prompt ?
can we adjust the heat ?
is there something we can take
to make this somehow easier
            to make it go away...

    the perfect
            debris

"do you have

an anti-inflammatory ?"

        pry off one more stray dog
    take out one more bad guy
but there's still tomorrow's agonies

"oh, and you said it was empty ?"

no further associations
outside the sacrifice

only the sacrifice ,
necessity for getting closer

the bees on the hill, returning ,
a whispered blessing

raw , raw , raw
cooked , burnt , smoking
measure of grain/oil

now the judge , the court
your vision of the justice-cloud on high
a goading dream...

someone arriving on horseback
obscuring the picture

nothing like
a major project
to set your teeth on edge

words cover the rawness
like walking on straw over shit

       the dear little crunch

where are the monks now , where did they go ?

     haunting the long sacred corridor

       the choir ,

       the song
               the

                          evening light

"keep doors
closed
at all
times"

for fire safety

more about feelings...

they are impossible to feel

against the enemy a God ?   Gods ?

who or what are we talking about ?

or is it just talk ,   just

not wasting paper   ,

the enflamed jambs

trying to get back to the night

desert ,
headlights cut the night
time to arrive

                          is final

              queer boulder , ice so blue

          a curtain dropping
      beyond the possibilities of our countrymen

   dirt road
  trailing billows of dust
erotic fantasies – better fragmentary
then never
              what you could possess , if only it is gone
              but nothing goes as planned
          what we wished for ,

                              what's that   ?

turning thirty today
or sixty

tango and tangle
of a serious life

sun behind clouds ,   muffled light
scudding quickly by as in a film

frozen ground , mountains , caves
water's drastic sucking swirl

        "everyday living ,   everything's alive..."

snow blows across tundra
("just what's seen")

penguins huddle
eggs between their toes

(for Hannah Fischer-Baum)

Explosion!
black smoke rising
in big bad plumes

a child in the next seat
masters her idiom

"*lets be honest*"

sun's heat
on & on & on

I'm lost
which doesn't mean how it sounds

crumpled blankets on the floor

distant sorry violin

"the" is *"one"*
"one" implies more
on the letters' humps

in our language
so terribly convincing

married
they could be so alone

     "who can help us

     with our human problems?"

sky crammed with birds
as it were

tiny growing light in the hill's notch

"I'm desperate"

I could climb El Capitan
I could dance till I drop

she's so smart & quiet
underneath that silver moon

not that there's anything wrong with that

pictures and text

links, lots of links

nothing as obvious as this
reject your first thought

he sells wine ,
she dismantles cities

choose another thought
or wait for the thought

that goes here

such round teeth   &   so   white
the brick path that leads to the house

smoke   &   rind of words

things are becoming
    very casual
                everywhere

        typing my strategic plan
        numbered items in prioritized order

    an alarmingly urgent
    tug on the line

belt's a notch
            too tight

        old man speaks with delight
        to interested young woman

    who or what
    is ever the matter

    neat blue shirt
            in both senses of the word

only two days ago
so we know there must be something wrong

the universe is broken and it is making me conscious
that things are getting rocky inside me

this is the beginning

here is the door through which I shall escape

arms of a chair
to lean on

"talk with your hands"

it's in my mind
I don't have to write it

no   hesitation

typing is visual
I can see the words in my mind

the ramifications of this are legion

Africa, where we come from

Who shall pay   ?

bright   yellow wall
in the background

for the dying in the foreground

dressed in black:

"you used a good word"

inside ,   our stuff

is consistent

tremor in the wrist
pursing of the lips
how heavy the teeth in the mouth
marvelous that they don't bite the tongue
stand still for a minute
your back against the wall
is regressive
it's spreading

it varies

no use

in a Sabbath

&

        no breaks

party plans at a bar

       "what happened to us ?"

       distill self and world

    six knots

seven days

       "what have we been doing ?"

     says an inchoate head

use what happens
it will help

the others , rich
inner life's a buzz

what you do
to be effective

this action
is where they meet

impact of the central theme
is not recorded

map of room or world
note the exits drawn in

see the clock tick

.... a bank of windows

"there's no inside or outside ?"

she thinks so , it's ok

but how did you get here ?

how do you get out   ?

who says so ?

conflict:

in & out   dark & light

inside , outside   upside down

the generally accepted format

the desire to flee is never

incorrect

a spade is never a spade

corners of the room where yellow walls meet

a dragon , tiny things on windowsill
outside the body is its meat , nearly dust

    &   no one can hurt you

    &

                        you don't need to care

it narrows to a point in absentia

          big lawn
      below
    hospital window

(for Michael Sawyer)

enclosed no more
in the social whirl

not even a short set
of useful words , even grunts ,

grins ,   grimaces ,   gestures

expressing human dilemma

where would we who remain stubbornly alive
find such a thing as you ?

outside the self's

self

(*for Michael Sawyer*)

a scientist ,   a therapist ,
    mother ,   a father

    bolt the doors
or open them

        how they're put together ,

taken apart

                "only just beginning the conversation"

ad infinitum
everywhere
for everyone but me

glass house
below green hills
beneath the tree a shadow

        a window
or
        a mirror
or
           a door

carry yourself across

                        "you are the others"

words capture experience

or are experience

"presence with a capital P"

we differ

for our views differ

we identify

or

perish

hardly leaving a trace

raw   &   raw

cooked   &   burnt

Adjudicate!!

like a river observed   going nowhere to the sea

dotted in white rhythms   dictated by wind

a lark

a loon
next to a naked lady

full effort
is full victory

$34.99
no small price to pay
to clean your clock

indicates something specific
like spit ,   all that's inside's out
in a fervent display of categories
in the zoo in Paris a sharp pain
&
Laurent ,   disgusted by the long rows of trees
a civilized city in memory

                                distorted by desire

        now & then means *not often*

                such as it is means *not so good*

witness the disjunction
that puts space between things
so that they are there
words that cannot last   :

                                animals in their cages

write it

&

rewrite it

&

rewrite it again

that which we witnessed

old man in purple pants
reading ads in the paper

       which side of the street ,   north

              south ,   east ,   west

Bush
        &
            Gough

     "once   they   start

          they   are   sure   to   end"

revelation reveals
the unknowable which ,
having been revealed ,
makes itself known

and herein likes a tale

misunderstood.....

speaking of which

as commanded

the silent letter *"h"*

the syllable *"ah"*

my *"I"* is yours

your *"you"* is mine

taken for the giving in the going

no time to think, no
time

                to think

is listening to the question

clearing his mind ,
Father Sonnborg
on Whidby

              rounds the lake

        taking
     the planet

                          into account

(for David Levy)

walnut paneled room
light falls in lines
across blinds

        a nephew

                                                  &

                                                                 his brain

"the experience

of being
or trying to be

human"

does medicine

consider

    a broader picture?

        "only individuals and groups"

Tiger Woods ,

    our exemplar of mental discipline

   wrapped in his cocoon of concentration

   the Gandhi of our day

        lets off steam with prurience

      "Esther, what would this tell us?"

   we really don't know

we're exploding

    with mental distress , it's normal

do not forget
the body

music is
a field

as much as silence
a rhythm

there are three or four
John Cage , music one

Murray Schaffer

children listening
in school

three parts
and we're done

sound
at the beginning

"every sound you hear"

those of us sitting here recognize
the statuette of the stable boy

holding a lantern
as if to point out to us

the way home
or that we are home

in exactly his light
how should we feel

about this
or that

who will tell us
to believe?

a cloud commands the distance
crisp air falls to the sea

        he had doubts
            about the shaman

      but who can deny
          the power of the sun

        on which we depend
absolutely
         we cannot imagine its absence

"original" point of view

              that the words float out from

trouble
in the financial markets

we debate
    messy world

what can we argue over ?
        what forms must our contentions take ?

who's off to market , who to jail , who *whee whee whees* all the way home ?

        money ,   these little crawling numbers made of light ,

our hope , our fear , our future

                        "money is special and serious"

                I am money , here is my hat

life is short ,   death is longer

        as *"something"* contains

                "nothing" &   vice versa

                            no rest for the counters

time for Olympic swimmers
in China, land beyond control

strokes not letters
pictures not sounds

"ways of thinking of Eastern peoples"

East , West , Middle
does anyone have a face?

not to have to wake to the struggle of a face

losing this...

                    "speak ,   memory ,   of time and loss

                              loss that is time"

hath no man a painted paradise
on his church wall

hath Chinese money
no less face

hath pictures
no words unwritten in the pen

the black ,   the blue
the brushed ink

on white sky-paper
the delicate cloud

harassed ,   *harangued*

in other ways

any form
land , heart , sword

the soul
the *"me"* I am

the *"mine"* I have
so dear in its distinction
its diminishment

listen
to the beginnings

listen
forget history   I don't know what happened

recount   what's surmised
so subject   to revision

as new facts   come to light
conflict is one's self ,   another

        conflict holds the world in place

this our system
what we are up against

the tools we have
as we walk away

test by fire
the litigant a lunatic

in his human situation
isolated   &   alone

negotiating with the devil
they come in

                              they sit down

some interesting language

is titrated

                                in broken trust
          find fluid rules

          visible as a supposed person

behind a cream-colored blind

          standing for a long while

          in the neighborhood

                                      the mask

               is who you really are

                    "I wonder

                              where's the real lawyer?"

conflict engraved on the tongue

one word is not another

                heal   &   herald

in Adam's park

            where there's injury ,   pardon ,

                            doubt ,   faith ,

          dark ,   light ,

                    despair ,   hope ,

sadness , joy ,   a thousand dreams

put to rest ,   April 26, 1997

they made rules   &   followed them

because there were rules   they violated them

stepping beyond   the designated guidelines

there was nowhere else to go

bright yellow cottonwoods

below deep green mountains

under pale blue skies

economic collapse

        means other numbers

                our naive hope

withdrawn to itself

        the colored future

          re-painted

in the way   one feels now

grasses ,   shades of brown &   beige

day &   night turn as before

at bottom ,   hope must rise ,

up , down's certain

        they made nothing from nothing

   in their lightness of mind

winning , they lost

real people   suffer hardship   their desire

      unanswered   their need

        unmet

              now as before   &   as ever

gouges with raw edges
unspoken unheard

             as hatred ,   elemental ,

    &

                           unchecked fear

"I'm not sure what I'm doing
I don't know what to do
I don't know why I'm here
I don't know where to go"

                always surprised to find
         again unknown
what I knew I knew
       or thought to know
  so well

slashed the
            conflict
to have been so well defeated   never to have surrendered
    my   bitterness   my   vow
alive   as life
so am brought   alive or dead

alive   &   dead

   a man   sits on a bench by a fountain

adobe buildings

as if the earth enfolds

lenticular clouds paint the sky phthalocyanine
as if arms or wings

flung open
not
moving
spots on my tie

Ralph   &   me

walking round   &

                              round in Sante Fe circles

some day
            an originary thought   to analyze the obvious

everything depends on   the rain

                                                            being
                                    at all

I'm absolutely

        nobody   ,

    and you ?

   nobody too ?

"*you , of all people , should know*"

modes of consternation
heart of the matter

        eternal "I am"

a border conflict
a gateless frontier

until you say so

alight with possibilities

ever aloft

looking for a storehouse world
online search
yields forked results

"you will read me   are reading me now"

    Ralph Steele ,   Ralph Steele

    weeps again in Vietnam

"I've been here before   ,

               breathing this poison"

bodies forth

     my darkness

           here on every touch

(for Ralph and all Vietnam soldiers)

torture confronts

the painful truth

that each has its price

&

there are reasons
always reason
laws

&   rules

peacefully

point the way to pain

hills become lover   ,

nemesis   ,   kin

whoever wrote the memo   remember what to protect
crack in the door   –   everything sucked out through the little opening

the photos ,   humiliation
being   one   the pride of   knowing one

what one proffers to be known
gone   when you don't sleep
crushed   when you can't breathe
out of control   ,   in a panic

who takes satisfaction
where oblivion's the matter
to be   wood
the body only bears so much

Akiva raked with combs
till his flesh tore off
climbed the final rung with "Hear!"

who pays the ultimate price

                    how can you sleep when you know   ?

forgive the sinner   ,   the powerful
make the strong weak

puncturing the soul ,   the will's
the flesh's weakness
when it depends on me
what   &   who   I am

                    erect now
                            a golden calf   :
                                        worship   ,
                    believe ,

                                        absolutely believe

pain comes in waves
they do & don't   relent
come in   ,   go out
as long as life abides

in time   ,   sensation
the heart detects its reasons

how much I depend
on standing up   ,   breathing air   ,   moving in time   ,   space

limbs   &   sinews   at rest
without pressure

how easily the world dissolves   absent this accustomed ease
an animal merely knows   no horror outside its life

what's worth protecting
to what extent

&

                    when

                                        does protection

            exceed that worth
                    its cost in pain

            overreaching
the value of existing

                    which always had
            a *not* in it ,

                    a knot ,   is there something

I should be dying for ?   *Can I*   *choose it ?*

no , it is   not right
therefore

            I must kill you

        or if not
                gouge out a hole

            in what you love
                    &
                        hold more dear

            than life   –   demeaning

that ,   a world dissolves in smoke ,   rising

            what's truly unbearable?
we   bear
what we   bear
&
                    go

shouting is not raping
raping is not stabbing
stabbing is not shooting dead
   dismembering   ,   beheading   ,   gouging out
the eyes ,   skinning alive
burning at the stake

for your actions of the past
for what you
profess
for your kinship   ,   your place of residence
your skin , your words , your possessions

for what I see as myself
my size   –   my meaning

I protect
follow the thread
          of my passion my will
                 "there's no forgetting this
                         ever"

fool myself with my argument
only to live and go on living
in its face

                        motivated
the rest comes behind ,
                                    pelicans following a boat

naked statements of fact

do not move me   they   are not so
I do not see
                my
                      enemy
                                  passion , not   human
his reasons are crimes
to make the world a nightmare
I have dreamed
to prevent which I sleep screaming

a nightmare I don't know I live

a world of limited possibilities
all artifice   &

                              smear

                    cutting off the simple
                                              music
               for tortured silence

     no statement possible
          I know   too much   to speak

          well ,   what used to be funny

                                   still is ,   falling down

when you least expect it   pushing a stone uphill

your beauty's source
a question
removed without reply

                    ,   *the world*   ,

                poured   into
                        the dark opening
                                that you are

                                            &   not

                    not given   ,
                    made
                    - & the difference ?-
                    thus unstable
                    pursuing itself ,
                    clawing
your second nature ,   culture ,   the totality of human products

    the earth throws off   like wind

sadly smoky   glazed with your absence

Lahore   ,   dozens
trapped in the rubble

two arrested – men
        get out of the car shooting

hundreds to hospital
"I was there on duty
        ..... the gunfire continued
                ..... the building collapsed"
at any time
can destroy our lives
or anyone
anywhere

                                which is ever the case

"Any hostile act
Upon our borders
Will be considered
An act of war"

Short range missiles
The treaty is done ,
She shouts
With a power behind her person

Welcome to you both
For the ominous
Challenge you face

break out or bust out
states go nuclear quickly
we must cool the situation
which is unprecedented

lest they fall into the hands.....
an immediate task
the hope   &   expectation

("we always say

those sorts of things")

good faith try
how we defend ourselves
containing ..... limiting .....

ratchet up , ratchet down

a new action for instance   North Korea , Libya , Syria ,
China , Russia , Japan   −

Painful   &   visible
At risk   ,   alone

Instructed by God

Both sons of Abraham

Christians   ,   Muslims

This dusty Lagos neighborhood

Torn apart or cleared
All are Christian

The lame are walking

And the blind are now seeing

"Why have I not
found favor in your eyes

to set the burden
of this entire people
on   me   now

Did I conceive this ?
Birth it ?
That you should tell me

'Carry them all the way home
as father ,   mother ,

And they cry at me , 'Give
us meat
to eat   ,   give us meat!'   Well

Kill me! Kill me if that is

How it is"

Humans and their Maker
have an undying basis

of conflict

the one beyond
the other inside

the one inside
the other beyond

Imperfect speech
Strains
to divide ,   unite

as they are as
they are not

Eve   .....   Cain   .....   Moses   .....
The divine   /   human   tangle
the head , the voice ,   saw daily   the wonders

68

yet moan   ,   murder ,   maraud

"And the relations
between God
and Abraham's descendents

are aimed
eventually

at resolving

this"

damage....

the whole of it lost it seems at sea....

no mere dis-
integration, a jewel-like collapse   ,

sea-change

in the soul
devolving distractions

all   a   fever   to   the   foam

Now

more

speak   -   you   -   too

Fulminating disentanglements
Blister-hot anger flagellants
Whipped upon the scene
No escaping
Relinquishment   ,   reverberation
Note-taking filaments in flash points

"While you were out"

The grate violation

Smoked the bulletin

....final shots already fired

Notional – crush the nation

Congress can't pass muster
Re-org in dilemma-pans
Whole realms of deadened refuge
And the cows come home only to be reborn

Whose health are we talking about anyway?
These little toady moves
I am mine for me who are they?
No more lights out
All over the place
Fall away

Maybe in death the defiance
All the machines can prevent that , can't they ?

Who heard of solution

In vitro ?

notions , barriers

in conflict resolve

to oppose , antipathy

    emotional lock down

of the aura , confounded

       gouge emulsions

       score a picture

nine times out of ten

engagement reveals

covert filaments

     wheat

      stone

       land

place name
heartache
toothache

land I love from the mountains
to the prairies
to the oceans white with foam

blood
under the flag
I imagine you are feeling

send you off on your way
try to stay with them

Kill them for their own good

Kill them for mine

kill the echo
live with the ghost

filaments   ,   fragments
falling charts dueling

                              statements

Why can't we just get along ?
How smooth out these trying feelings ?

bird-tracks

in the sand
                              scream
                        of the
                                          absent
                                                   bird
searching for food or mate
   a body,   a
                        soul

conflict is

                                            relational

how I am

I am emotional

I don't know what you are

he / she / they / there is no us / we

                                     conflict's force in the pronouns

        differing relations

        sexual particulars

        differing types , vantage points , shouting distances

        singular   or   otherwise

        head , heart

        gouged , flagellated , foamed

the emotion   would I rather die?

In presence of others I
Relent   ,   in presence of others I

                    Forsake

                    in such presence ache,   demur

                    wilt   , dissolve , I cannot be

        so resolve to inhabit a larger darkness
        whole radial knobs ,   fate of us / we

      twists in the wind
                    undying harbinger of my whole fight
against wagering my soul for the dirt
                    in which it's moistened

In others' presence   all the cloth in the world

gathered together in a clot   harsh words of rebuke would kill

my minus dilemma   ,   my weight

"When I'm afraid I....."

which war was it when

                           food was scarce   ,

       I climbed
     over the bodies and   bloodied
                         body
                                parts
looking for what   to eat

filaments ,   fragments   , little vague vignettes
when there's no feeling
only a bar
around the heart
amidst the birdsong   &   silence   &   birthday

of the soul

a day in the life
"Each day the fury, the desperation..."
can't get along ,   can't get going   out of here to that

source of the stream between boulders
womb – fear ,   desire ,   chagrin
guy outside the bar raving
kids coming out of the storefront tutoring place
with your knees together   ,   your feet apart
trees   , hills   &   gray sky

outside the rehab center

how you make a life
of silence

against the scream
why did you do that?

how could I not
have done that

what's done is done
what is is

does it
make any difference?

what's difference?

angel on the garden wall   looks out   where red leaves fallen
make a carpet   &   a view   this white sky ,   full of cold
ease ,   barren trees   my endless carping word

in the role you are in

reactions , emotions , judgments

write that down
you are not lost

where are you ?
how is your head ?

broken , bruised ?
is there blood ?

is that the sacrifice ,

the movement   back   &   forth
up   &   down   the trees'

quivering
in the large group one word

       fear , reaction , impasse ....

Ineffective

"When I feel an afflictive emotion I..."

write it down   ,   I explain it
to myself   ,   to you

then there is
a monastery door   ,   it is open   ,
closed   don't know what's
on the   other side

floating leaf
in no one's hand or fist...

national news
one more big mess I can't explain   ,
can't fix   ,   can't
tolerate

so you say   ,   you say so
you talk with your hands
lean on your chair

"this is sacred work"

the worst thing that could happen....
the bowl of the bell afloat

                              upon the green sea
          the hollow men , the journeymen
ambient noise ,   scorn ,   shouting ,   abuse ,   scuffle
that which ,   witnessed , we witness
that which we feel or are or do

the mist in which bare trees
stand as if watchful
of funerals ,   dim doings ,
visible as are a person

the one not yet here
whom we fear

About the Author

Norman Fischer is a Zen priest and abbot who lives in Muir Beach, California. Active in San Francisco Bay Area poetry circles since the 1970's, he has been publishing prose and poetry ever since. He is executor of the Philip Whalen literary estate.

About Chax Press

Chax Press has been publishing books in Tucson Arizona since 1984. Recent works include books by Samuel Ace & Maureen Seaton, Leslie Scalapino, Charles Olson, Mark Weiss, Drum Hadley, fine letterpress chapbooks by Anne Waldman and Eileen Myles, and many more. We have published 137 books to date, and look forward to many more in the next several years. Please visit our web site at chax.org, and look for our books at the Small Press Distribution site, spdbooks.org. Chax Press has received support from the Tucson Pima Arts Council, the Arizona Commission on the Arts, and the National Endowment for the Arts, but the greatest part of our support comes from individual donors. To join our supporters, please visit our web donation page at http://chax.org/donate.htm.